TO LEARN THE FUTURE

TO LEARN THE FUTURE

POEMS FOR TEACHERS

Edited by
Jane Cooper
Lilias Fraser
Kate Hendry
Samuel Tongue

Scottish **Poetry** Library

Polygon

This edition published in 2021 by the Scottish Poetry Library
5 Crichton's Close, Edinburgh EH8 8DT and
Polygon, an imprint of Birlinn Ltd
West Newington House, 10 Newington Road
Edinbrugh EH9 1QS

9 8 7 6 5 4 3 2 1

First published in 2018 by the Scottish Poetry Library

www.scottishpoetrylibrary.org.uk
www.polygonbooks.co.uk

ISBN 978 1 84697 554 7

Typeset in Verdigris MVB by Polygon, Edinburgh
Cover design by Polygon, based on the original series design by
Gerry Cambridge.

The publishers are grateful for partner support towards the
costs of this anthology.

CONTENTS

III. BALANCING IT ALL

IV. NEW EVERY MORNING

All our lives we remember our teachers. A good teacher knows it is not lessons they teach but students. This gem of a book is for everyone, and I hope it will be enjoyed as much by the PE and Physics teachers as by those who deliver *A Midsummer Night's Dream*. Here are texts that talk to each other and to the reader – you, dear teacher – using the language of poetry to investigate, to remember, and to celebrate education. Whether you savour them in your lunch hour or after hours, these poems will hold open the door, and make you welcome.

The wonderful thing about this book is that it has no agenda, no policy directive. No grading required. No planning necessary. What a relief! Poems to bounce off, to inspire, to offer moments of recognition, a necessary pause. Poems to ring through good days and bad. These poems are not teaching aids, but life aids; not set texts but subtexts. This gift is not homework but heart work. Please turn over the page and begin!

Jackie Kay
Scottish Makar

FROM THE EDITORS

Welcome to the second edition of *To Learn the Future: Poems for Teachers*. Come in and make yourself at home. Grab a cuppa and a chocolate biscuit. This little book is a gift to you, whether you are stepping into the classroom for the first time, have years of experience under your belt, or simply value the teachers and teaching that have contributed so much to making you who you are.

The classroom is a microcosm of individuals' lives, triumphs and passions, their insecurities and fears and, more often than you might think, their unalloyed joys. The editors have worked hard to find poems that reflect this kaleidoscopic environment with its myriad voices and perspectives.

Where possible, we've included original languages as well as translations; in other cases, the original language is English but the poem explores a rich cultural identity. We hope that the poems will conjure a moment of recognition or insight; even if you find only one or two that speak to you, we trust that they will buddy you through difficult days or open doors to better times.

We've also included space for reflection, and provided prompts but please note: This. Is. NOT. More. Homework!

As the Scottish Makar, Jackie Kay, says in her foreword, this book holds poems to 'bounce off, to inspire, to offer moments of recognition, a necessary pause.' These spaces are for you to spin thoughts and phrases, worries and ideas and, perhaps, to see a way through: not homework, but (in Jackie's words) 'heartwork'.

We are proud that the second edition of this book is again supported by professional education organisations, including the General Teaching Council of Scotland (GTCS), and teaching unions: we have significant support from the Educational Institute of Scotland (EIS), and the Association of Headteachers and Deputes Scotland (AHDS). Their enthusiasm, interest, and care for the project have been considerable. You will find more details about these organisations at the back of the book: they, like this book of poems, are here for you at every stage of your teaching career.

We're grateful in particular to the librarians of the Scottish Poetry Library, whose ingenious searches provided a wealth of poems, and we are very grateful to the poets and publishers who gave permission to use the poems we selected; in many cases they reduced or waived fees, and wrote notes to welcome readers to their poems. We also thank the teachers who added comments charting how some of the poems resonated with them, and for readers who helped us seek out poems for the first edition; they are listed at the end of the book.

Finally, thank you to Edward Crossan and the team at Polygon for steering this book all the way to publication.

Jane Cooper
Lilias Fraser
Kate Hendry
Samuel Tongue

I. STARTING OUT

THE DOOR

Go and open the door.
    Maybe outside there's
    a tree, or a wood,
    a garden,
    or a magic city.

Go and open the door.
    Maybe a dog's rummaging.
    Maybe you'll see a face,
or an eye,
or the picture
    of a picture.

Go and open the door.
    If there's a fog
    it will clear.

Go and open the door.
    Even if there's only
    the darkness ticking,
    even if there's only
    the hollow wind,

even if
    nothing
        is there,
go and open the door.

At least
there'll be
a draught.

Miroslav Holub
Translated from the Czech by
Ian Milner

ODE TO TEACHERS

I remember
the first day,
how I looked down,
hoping you wouldn't see
me,
and when I glanced up,
I saw your smile
shining like a soft light
from deep inside you.

'I'm listening,' you encourage us.
'Come on!
Join our conversation,
let us hear your neon certainties,
thorny doubts, tangled angers,'
but for weeks I hid inside.

I read and reread your notes
praising
my writing,
and you whispered,
'We need you

and your stories
and questions
that like a fresh path
will take us to new vistas.'

Slowly, your faith grew
into my courage
and for you –
instead of handing you
a note or apple or flowers –
I raised my hand.

I carry your smile
and faith inside like I carry
my dog's face,
my sister's laugh,
creamy melodies,
the softness of sunrise,
steady blessings of stars,
autumn smell of gingerbread,
the security of a sweater on a chilly day.

Pat Mora

HOW TO BE A TEACHER

First,
despair of what you know.
It will not be enough.
It is not the right kind.
You are as unprepared
as you fear.

Let the things you know
fall out of your hands
and shatter on the floor.
They will not fall
in neat pieces
but blow away instantly
in dust.

This dust will coat your hands,
your students' faces. It will get
into your lungs and make you cough.
It will get into your eyes, where it sparkles
and refracts.

Bring stories in your open hands.
There will be questions like, what
is a devil? How many quotes
are we required to use? Do you want

a revolution? Would you, personally, go
to the site of one? When is that essay due,
again, and what is it about?

When one of them tells you he cannot write,
ask him to draw. And when he draws a fish,
look at the fish. And when he writes about the fish,
take what you know about him now, as mysterious
as what you did not know before, and hold it.

Love your students. Surprise and disappoint
them. They will do the same for you.
They will write you on New Year's Eve.
One will send a picture of her bandaged head.
One will send an essay for revision.
One will ask you, do you understand how I feel?

Take what you know now and hold it close.
Make it into pottery, something beautiful.
Next time you begin a class, hold it in your hands
on the very first day, when you wish
you were a plumber or a politician or
anything but this – and let it drop.
And so begin.

Rebecca Lynne Fullan

I love the way this poem suggests that knowledge is created in collaboration. In this particular American context, students may be older and teaching contact different; but the sense of shared discovery and learning is the same for all of us. We learn how to teach through and with our pupils – acknowledging what we don't know, building answers together. For me, the joy of teaching is in building relationships and this poem captures the rewards, surprises and challenges of that process. We learn to handle unexpected questions and confidences with a boundaried empathy.

Secondary English teacher,
Edinburgh

FEAR OF THE LITANY

I remember thinking I teach every grade
every classroom that means eventually
I'm supposed to know every name.
How the hell do I do that?

I ask some other teachers.
No one has any tricks, they just say oh,
you'll get the hang of it, you will.

But that's because maybe I look like a teacher,
or a smart person, or adult enough to handle it.
I'm faking it, I can't do this, I've got them
all faked out.

Barely the end of September,
and Terry sees me kissing her
before I get out of the car.
Now I have to deal with this.
I may want to work here longer
than the end of the pay period.
Shit. So I go in, and I
wait till the end of the day.

Yeah, I saw you with her.
She's my lover.
Yeah, well I figured she wasn't just a good friend,
since my wife kisses me goodbye on the lips,
not my friends.
He was already being himself, Terry, teasing.
So I blurted it out, my fear of the litany
of names, my fear of faking
being a teacher and he said
Oh but you are.
You're right for this place and
you're right on schedule, breaking down.
You've got it, I've watched you with them.

What about technique, philosophy, content?
You might want to get your kiss
before the parking lot,
but even that…they trust you.
That's all it takes.

Maggie Kazel

REFLECTION

How do you decide which parts of your life to share with your pupils and colleagues? What would happen if something was shared by accident?

ON FIRST KNOWING YOU'RE A TEACHER

Robert's not coming in, my boss tells me.
I'm sitting sweating in a windowless office,
a stack of résumés eye-balling me, stinking
up the desk – I'm first screener and sleepy
in this stuffy box. *Would you be able to lead
a workshop on résumé writing?* I'm 22
and my own résumé got me the most boring
gig at Jobs for Youth – Chicago. Some of the 'youth'
I'd be teaching are nearly my age, but there are
windows, and people, in that classroom
so I nearly yell, *yes!* 30 students look at me
and 45 minutes later look *to* me and I'm hooked.
And I'm floating and anchored at the same time.
For the first time. And I'm whole and broken
open. And I'm spinning and stunned still.

Peter Kahn

When I first started teaching, I thought
my students could see my heart on my sleeve.
I thought they could read the footnotes of
a body splayed open as a book.
I felt embarrassed to have such a
visible heart; there was something shameful about
the whole goopy mess, its ungovernable pulsations,
its lightning blush. It seemed none of my students
had a heart like mine; their hearts were bundled
in their baggy sweatshirts like a packed lunch.
I stood up there on the first day and
dug my hands into my pockets, thinking I
could hide my heart and its waywardness.
I slumped my shoulders, faced
the blackboard, shouted from
behind the projection screen.
But wherever I stood, my heart sparked
like a disco ball, doing
its unmistakeable kaleidoscope dance.
I went to my supervisor: I'm so
embarrassed, I said. I think my students
are judging me harshly. They've probably
never seen such a heart before.
She shuffled papers, looked at
the results of my classroom observation.

She said, Well, the best you can do
is be a role model. Maybe they've never had the chance to
learn about the heart. Try teaching it
the same way you teach grammar.
So I went back to class, and returned to
the living pulse of the text:
I glimpsed the luminous globe behind
the poem's dark ribs, felt its warmth streaming
through form, through syntax, through meter's
tangled orchard. I saw the poem as a latticework
interwoven with sun. Each sentence was
parsed by the light.
On the desks we drummed
the heartbeat of the iambs. My heart led an
orchestra of small flowers.

Nina Pick

*Reminded me of my early days, when I assumed the children could
sense my nerves, knew when I made a mistake and could tell that I
would beat myself up when they left. Then when I started to be me and
not someone else teaching, it got easier, just like this.*

Richard, primary teacher,
West Lothian

INSTRUCTIONS ON NOT GIVING UP

More than the fuchsia funnels breaking out
of the crabapple tree, more than the neighbour's
almost obscene display of cherry limbs shoving
their cotton candy-colored blossoms to the slate
sky of Spring rains, it's the greening of the trees
that really gets to me. When all the shock of white
and taffy, the world's baubles and trinkets, leave
the pavement strewn with the confetti of aftermath,
the leaves come. Patient, plodding, a green skin
growing over whatever winter did to us, a return
to the strange idea of continuous living despite
the mess of us, the hurt, the empty. Fine then,
I'll take it, the tree seems to say, a new slick leaf
unfurling like a fist to an open palm, I'll take it all.

Ada Limón

REFLECTION

This poem is full of colours and tastes. Find, or go out and take, a picture that you think goes with the poem. Eat a food that's in the poem, or one that brings you a rush of joy.

II. GETTING TO KNOW

ISN'T MY NAME MAGICAL?

Nobody can see my name on me.
My name is inside
and all over me, unseen
like other people also keep it.
Isn't my name magical?

My name is mine only.
It tells me I am individual,
the one special person it shakes
when I'm wanted.

Even if someone else answers
for me, my message hangs in the air
haunting others, till it stops
with me, the right name.
Isn't your name and my name magic?

If I'm with hundreds of people
and my name gets called,
my sound switches me on to answer
like it was my human electricity.

My name echoes across the playground,
it comes, it demands my attention,
I have to find out who calls,

who wants me for what.
My name gets blurted out in class,
it is terror, at a bad time,
because somebody is cross.

My name gets called in a whisper,
I am happy, because
my name may have touched me
with a loving voice.
Isn't your name and my name magic?

James Berry

A BOY'S HEAD

In it there is a space-ship
and a project
for doing away with piano lessons.

And there is
Noah's ark,
which shall be first.

And there is
an entirely new bird,
an entirely new hare,
an entirely new bumble-bee.

There is a river
that flows upwards.

There is a multiplication table.

There is anti-matter.

And it just cannot be trimmed.

I believe
that only what cannot be trimmed
is a head.

There is much promise
in the circumstance
that so many people have heads.

Miroslav Holub
Translated from the Czech by
Ian Milner

REFLECTION

What surprising things have you found in pupils' heads? What unexpected and joyful things are in your head?

SLOW READER

He can make a sculpture
and fabulous machines,
invent games, tell jokes,
give solemn, adult advice –
but he is slow to read.
When I take him on my knee
with his Ladybird book
he gazes into the air,
sighing and shaking his head
like an old man
who knows the mountains
are impassable.

He toys with words,
letting them go cold
as gristly meat,
until I relent
and let him wriggle free:
a fish returning
to its element,
or a white-eyed colt – shying
from the bit – who sees

that if he takes it
in his mouth
he'll never run
quite free again.

Vicki Feaver

CLANN A CLUICH, SGOIL
ACHADH NAN SIAN

glac am ball seo
tha saoghal ann

cumaidh mise
mo shoaghal dlùth rium

tha mise cunntas nan saoghal
am barraibh mo mheòir

ni mise sgàirt agus
dannsa tromh'n àile
tha do chruinne gun fheum dhomh

tha fàinne nam dhòrnsa, ach
có dh'iarradh fàinne

eadar dàghreim tha ròpa
nathair nan cleas
nathair nan briathar
nathair nan òran

aonghas macneacail

CHILDREN PLAYING,
ACHNASHEEN SCHOOL

catch this ball
there's a world in it

I'll keep
my world close to me

I'm counting the worlds
in the tips of my fingers

I'll shout, and
dance through the air,
I don't need your globe

I clutch a ring, but
who needs a ring

two hands hold a rope
the snake of games
the snake of words
the snake of songs

aonghas macneacail

ON TURNING TEN

The whole idea of it makes me feel
like I'm coming down with something,
something worse than any stomach ache
or the headaches I get from reading in bad light –
a kind of measles of the spirit,
a mumps of the psyche,
a disfiguring chicken pox of the soul.

You tell me it is too early to be looking back,
but that is because you have forgotten
the perfect simplicity of being one
and the beautiful complexity introduced by two.
But I can lie on my bed and remember every digit.
At four I was an Arabian wizard.
I could make myself invisible
by drinking a glass of milk a certain way.
At seven I was a soldier, at nine a prince.

But now I am mostly at the window
watching the late afternoon light.
Back then it never fell so solemnly
against the side of my tree house,
and my bicycle never leaned against the garage
as it does today,
all the dark blue speed drained out of it.

This is the beginning of sadness, I say to myself,
as I walk through the universe in my sneakers.
It is time to say goodbye to my imaginary friends,
time to turn the first big number.

It seems only yesterday I used to believe
there was nothing under my skin but light.
If you cut me I could shine.
But now when I fall upon the sidewalks of life,
I skin my knees. I bleed.

Billy Collins

GLENIS

The teacher says:

Why is it, Glenis,
Please answer me this,
The only time
You ever stop talking in class.
Is if I ask you
Where's the Khyber Pass?
Or when was the Battle of Waterloo?
Or what is nine times three?
Or how do you spell
Mississippi?
Why is it, Glenis,
The only time you are silent
Is when I ask you a question?

And Glenis says:

Allan Ahlberg

REFLECTION

What helps you communicate with pupils who are harder to reach?

HAMID

'O'm finking,' says Hamid.
It's 'I'm thinking,' says the teacher.
'Nah man, that's wot you say 'cos you're a teacher
an' you're middoo class, but O'm not so I sez O'm finking.
It's like you goin' on about da geezer wrote
da macbef play, yeh. You sez to us, you sez,
'Don't get put off by da crappy langwidge,
'cos it's changin' alla time – da macbef langwidge
is like word-up on the street back then.
So wot I is sayin is O'm finkin, an' you
'ave to go along wiv dat 'cos it's the langwidge
changin', innit?'

Rowland Molony

CONVERSATION WITH THE ART TEACHER
(a Translation Attempt)

Shit and good my education. Hearing teachers not see potential. This is my confusion life, 90s hearing teachers not think I can become artist because of deafness but funny thing, Deaf girl does GCSE art in six months and go on to get degree. I have proved many wrongs. I am costume designer, teacher, artist. At school I said, 'I want to be a costume designer.' Teacher says, 'I can't'. I can't? So harsh. My father, hearing, signs. Says I can follow dream and lucky me, I did. Proving people wrong is great but tiring. Was I born deaf? You asking a lot of questions! OK, yes, in Somaliland, I was about two, meningitis. Seven other children in my hospital ward, all died. My father worked around Europe and took me with him. English hospital saved me. I still know some Somali sign. Wait, you write down what I say, how? You know BSL has no grammar structure? How you write me when I am visual? Me, into fashion, expression in colour. How will someone reading this see my feeling?

Raymond Antrobus

SAM BUT DIFFERENT

Sam but different

Ha'in, fae da start, mair as ee wye o spaekin,
o makkin sense o things, we learn ta fit
whit we say ta whit's lippened. Takk pity apö dem
at's born ta wan tongue: dem at nivver preeve
maet fae idder tables. Raised wi twa languages
is unconscious faestin: twa wyes o tinkin.
Een extends da tidder; can shaa wis anidder wirld
yet foo aa wirlds ir jöst da sam, but different.

Same but different

Having, from the start, more than one way of speaking,
of making sense of things, we learn to fit
what we say to what's expected. Take pity on those
born to one tongue: those who never taste even a morsel
from other tables. Raised with two languages
is unconscious feasting: two ways of thinking.
One extends the other; can show us another world
yet how all worlds are just the same, but different.

Christine De Luca

[44]

PEOPLE EQUAL

Some people shoot up tall.
Some hardly leave the ground at all.
          Yet – people equal. Equal.

One voice is a sweet mango.
Another is a non-sugar tomato.
          Yet – people equal. Equal.

Some people rush to the front.
Others hang back, feeling they can't.
          Yet – people equal. Equal.

Hammer some people, you meet a wall
Blow hard on others they fall.
          Yet – people equal. Equal.

One person will aim at a star.
For another. A hilltop is *too far*.
          Yet – people equal. Equal.

Some people get on with their show.
Others never get on the go.
          Yet – people equal. Equal.

James Berry

صدا

من از سر زمین غریب می‌آیم
با کوله بار بیگانه‌گی ام بر دوش
و سرود خاموشی ام برلب
من یونس صدایم را
آن‌گاه که از رودبار حادثه می‌گذشتم
دیدم

درکامی نهنگی فرورفت
و تمام هستی من
در صدایم بود

شهر کابل
دسامبر ۱۹۸۹

MY VOICE

I come from a distant land
with a foreign knapsack on my back
with a silenced song on my lips

As I travelled down the river of my life
I saw my voice
(like Jonah)
swallowed by a whale

And my very life lived in my voice

Partaw Naderi
Translated from the Farsi-Dari
by Sarah Maguire *and* Yama
Yari

A BOOK CLOSER TO HOME

Every Saturday mum took us to the library.
We dispersed into different parts of the room,

craving this yellow smell of bound paper
and a peep into lives we did not live –
where tea was not chai, but dinner.

Mum sat in the Urdu section,
soon dissolving into a magazine
full of squiggles that only made sense to her.

Her large almond eyes smiled.
Her soft fingers turned the pages,
pausing while she glanced at us with motherly duty.

We sat with our books on the carpeted floor,
following the curves and lines of English
with our fingertips,

the red signs on the mahogany shelves
silencing our tongue.

                              Nabila Jameel

CLASSROOM POLITICS

They will not forgive us
These girls
Sitting in serried rows
Hungry for attention
Like shelves of unread books
If we do not
Make the world new for them
Teach them to walk
Into the possibilities
Of their own becoming
Confident in their exploring.

They will not forget
If we do not use
Our often-surrendered positions
On the front line
To wage war against
The subtle hordes of male historians
Who constantly edit female experience
And endlessly anthologise
Their own achievements.

They will not accept
The old excuses of their foremothers
If they grow up to find
That we have betrayed them.

Fiona Norris

What do you feel you owe your pupils? What must you get right for them?

DUNCAN GETS EXPELLED

There are three big boys from primary seven
who wait at the main school gate with stones
in their teeth and names in their pockets.
Every day the three big boys are waiting.
'There she is. Into her, boys. Hey, Sambo.'

I dread the bell ringing, and the walk home.
My best friend is scared of them and runs off.
Some days they shove a mud pie into my mouth.
'That's what you should eat,' and make me eat it.
Then they all look into my mouth, prodding a stick.

I'm always hoping we get detention.
I'd love to write 'I will be better' 400 times.
The things I do? I pull Agnes MacNamara's hair.
Or put a ruler under Rhona's bum and ping it back
till she screams; or I make myself sick in the toilet.

Until the day the headmaster pulls me out,
asking all about the three big boys.
I'm scared to open my mouth.
But he says, 'You can tell me, is it true?'
So out it comes, making me eat the mud pies.

Two of them got lines for the whole of May.
But he got expelled, that Duncan MacKay.

Jackie Kay

LISTEN

Written for the Children's Panel, to encourage
new voluntary members, 2012

Trouble is not my middle name.
It is not what I am.
I was not born for this.
Trouble is not a place
though I am in it deeper than the deepest wood
and I'd get out of it (who wouldn't?) if I could.

Hope is what I do not have in hell –
not without good help, now. Could you
listen, listen hard and well
to what I cannot say except by what I do?

And when you say I do it for badness
this much is true:
I do it for badness done to me before
any badness that I do to you.

Hard to unfankle this.
But you can help me.
Maybe.
Loosen
all these knots and really listen.
I cannot plainly tell you this, but, if you care,
then – beyond all harm and hurt –
real hope is there.

Liz Lochhead

YOUR DAD DID WHAT?

Where they have been, if they have been away,
or what they've done at home, if they have not –
you make them write about the holiday.
One writes *My Dad did*. What? Your Dad did what?

That's not a sentence. Never mind the bell.
We stay behind until the work is done.
You count their words (you who can count and spell);
all the assignments are complete bar one

and though this boy seems bright, that one is his.
He says he's finished, doesn't want to add
anything, hands it in just as it is.
No change. *My Dad did*. What? What did his Dad?

You find the 'E' you gave him as you sort
through reams of what this girl did, what that lad did,
and read the line again, just one 'e' short:
This holiday was horrible. My Dad did.

Sophie Hannah

This simple, beautiful poem captures the poignancy, experienced all too often in teaching, of clarity when we glimpse the real lives of our children and young people, in school for just 16% of the hours of their school-age lives.

Angela Bell, DHT Secondary

REFLECTION

Can you recall a moment of startling insight into a pupil's life?

EVERY LINE IS IMAGINARY

A jumble of bodies bobbing and shifting.
There is sweat, and rhythm, and pain.
One turn from the end.
He is last.
I wish he already knew
that finishing lines don't really exist,
that the trick is not stopping.
But he is twelve years old,
full of summer
and, would you believe it, coming up fast.

William Letford

SCAFFOLDING

They need to trust you
describe their reasoning
in detail. Each premise
must be laid bare.

'Why did you do that?

Where did *that* number
come from?'

I follow each step
searching for the wrong idea
the mistaken concept.

Sometimes, all I gift
is one new thought like . . .
'Dividing *can* make
a number bigger'
and it's as if I see
their minds inflate.

It's like blowing air
into someone else's lungs.
You have to stop
as soon as you can.

You need them
to breathe again
– all on their own.

Eveline Pye

'I see their minds inflate' – a line that wonderfully summed up those
fleeting and always to be savoured moments when you can see the
children learn. That's why we teach, not to go to meetings but help
them all grow.

Richard, primary teacher,
West Lothian

THE DOMINIE'S ANNUAL
IMPROVEMENT PLAN

The Curriculum:
Aa the stuff
the bairns
hivtae ken.

Meeting Learners' Needs:
Helpin the bairns
hou tae lairn
aa the stuff.

Improving Learners' Experiences:
The bairns haein
a braw time
lairnin aa the stuff.

Improvements in Performance:
The bairns daein weill
at mindin
aa the stuff.

Improvements Through Self-Evaluation:
Tae see oursels
as the bairns see us
teaching them aa the stuff.

William Hershaw

III . BALANCING IT ALL

INTRODUCTION TO POETRY

I ask them to take a poem
and hold it up to the light
like a colour slide

or press an ear against its hive.

I say drop a mouse into a poem
and watch him probe his way out,

or walk inside the poem's room
and feel the walls for a light switch.

I want them to waterski
across the surface of a poem
waving at the author's name on the shore.

But all they want to do
is tie the poem to a chair with rope
and torture a confession out of it.

They begin beating it with a hose
to find out what it really means.

Billy Collins

This poem made me, as a former English teacher, smile. I liked its humorous contrast of the teaching of a delicate appreciation of poetry and all its nuance, with the temptation to resort to brutal, joyless over-analysis of it in pursuit of 'the correct answer'. Encouraging our students to look, listen and feel their way to understanding poems and the thoughts and emotions that their authors might have been trying to stir in us, boosts their enjoyment of poetry – both reading it and writing it.

Andrea Bradley, former
secondary teacher

Nothing. When we realised you weren't here
we sat with our hands folded on our desks
in silence, for the full two hours

    Everything. I gave an exam worth
    40 percent of the grade for this term
    and assigned some reading due today
    on which I'm about to hand out a quiz
    worth 50 percent

Nothing. None of the content of this course
has value or meaning
Take as many days off as you like:
any activities we undertake as a class
I assure you will not matter either to you or me
and are without purpose

    Everything. A few minutes after we began last time
    a shaft of light suddenly descended and an angel
    or other heavenly being appeared
    and revealed to us what each woman or man must do
    to attain divine wisdom in this life and
    the hereafter

This is the last time the class will meet
before we disperse to bring the good news to all people
on earth.

Nothing. When you are not present
how could something significant occur?

Everything. Contained in this classroom
is a microcosm of human experience
assembled for you to query and examine and ponder
This is not the only place such an opportunity has been
gathered

but it was one place

And you weren't here

Tom Wayman

'What *did I miss?'* wouldn't have stung so much, would it? So, this
wildly-exaggerated (unspoken) frustration is not directed at the pupil
asking for help to catch up after absence; it's laughing away our own
frustration, teasing ourselves for letting that casual wording hit a raw
nerve.

Jane Cooper, former
secondary teacher, Edinburgh

REFLECTION

What might your pupils say that would unintentionally upset you?
What do you secretly wish you could say in return?

CZWARTA NAD RANEM

Godzina z nocy na dzień.
Godzina z boku na bok.
Godzina dla trzydziestoletnich.

Godzina uprzątnięta pod kogutów pianie.
Godzina, kiedy ziemia zapiera się nas.
Godzina, kiedy wieje od wygasłych gwiazd.
Godzina a-czy-po-nas-nic-nie-pozostanie.

Godzina pusta.
Godzina czcza.
Dno wszystkich innych godzin.

Nikomu nie jest dobrze o czwartej nad ranem.
Jeśli mrówkom jest dobrze o czwartej nad ranem
– pogratulujmy mrówkom. I niech przyjdzie piąta,
o ile mamy dalej żyć.

Wisława Szymborska

FOUR A.M.

The hour between night and day.
The hour between toss and turn.
The hour of thirty-year-olds.

The hour swept clean for roosters' crowing.
The hour when the earth takes back its warm embrace.
The hour of cool drafts from extinguished stars.
The hour of do-we-vanish-too-without-a-trace.

Empty hour.
Hollow. Vain.
Rock bottom of all the other hours.

No one feels fine at four a.m.
If ants feel fine at four a.m.,
we're happy for the ants. And let five a.m. come
if we've got to go on living.

> Wisława Szymborska
> *Translated from Polish by*
> Stanisław Barańczak and
> Clare Cavanagh

REFLECTION

List, or draw, the things that fly around your head when you can't sleep. Put the list or picture away for a few days. When you come back to it, cross out the things that are now solved, or that seem small and silly in daylight. Pick one thing that is still there. What one action could you take now that would help you start to solve this?

SOMETIMES

Sometimes things don't go, after all,
from bad to worse. Some years, muscadel
faces down frost; green thrives; the crops don't fail,
sometimes a man aims high, and all goes well.

A people sometimes will step back from war;
elect an honest man; decide they care
enough, that they can't leave some stranger poor.
Some men become what they are born for.

Sometimes our best efforts do not go
amiss; sometimes we do as we meant to.
The sun will sometimes melt a field of sorrow
that seemed hard frozen: may it happen for you.

                    Anon

THE PEACE OF WILD THINGS

When despair for the world grows in me
and I wake in the night at the least sound
in fear of what my life and my children's lives may be,
I go and lie down where the wood drake
rests in his beauty on the water, and the great heron feeds.
I come into the peace of wild things
who do not tax their lives with forethought
of grief. I come into the presence of still water.
And I feel above me the day-blind stars
waiting with their light. For a time
I rest in the grace of the world, and am free.

Wendell Berry

REFLECTION

Recall a time when an encounter with nature helped you or gave you strength.

END OF YEAR EXAM

A floorboard creaks
but mostly it's like the sea,
old grain flowing like dark water.
Overhead, through tall windows,
the breeze catches clouds.
It is a voyage this, just the beginning,
but they are moving away,
sails are filling,
they are beating time on paper with ink,
the destination a dream,
the impetus all that matters,
the keel dragging free of shale.

Hugh McMillan

LEAVING TEACHING

When I walk into Year 3 each Tuesday morning
they always have their mouthpieces in their hands.
Who would like to buzz I say and we begin,
back and forward, call and response.
Let's pretend we're on a motorbike.
Let's pretend we are bees.
At the end, one of the girls hugs me and says
I'm really glad you're our music teacher,
and a boy says *where did you get your shoes from Miss,*
they're well cool, and I'll admit it, my heart soars a little
and the idea of leaving it behind in July,
of never having to pull a perfect Bb from the air
with my voice for the class to copy, no not the air,
after all these years, it feels as if that note lives
in my chest, I've carried it for so long, the idea
of never giving this to anyone again feels terrible.
Thank god for the afternoon session, when a girl
tells me she's bored, and a boy leans on his trumpet
then runs around it in a circle, so the mouthpiece gets stuck,
and the whole lesson feels like a battle, the class
talking through my recap of crotchets and minims,
although it's not the whole class, it's never the whole class,
just a constant few, talking their lives away,
whispering I don't know what, my mind can't
reach back across the years to think what it was

that we used to whisper behind our desks.
Today there was a fight at lunchtime and rudeness
to the dinner ladies, who come in outraged
and wanting retribution. I've been asked to save
the Year 5 end-of-term performance
of Joseph and the Amazing Technicolour Dreamcoat
which will involve gathering around the piano
and an explanation of the head and chest voice.
Two boys won't stop shoving each other as another
tells me over and over again *my valves are sticking*,
actually he says *my vowels are sticking*,
his hand waving in the air, *my vowels my vowels*,
my vowels are sticking and I admit it, I lose my temper
and give up all at the same time, it's like being a balloon
ready to burst and then being popped, it is a terrible thing,
this moving on, this giving in.

Kim Moore

REFLECTION

If you were to leave, or to finish, teaching, what would you miss most?

CHANGED

For months he taught us, stiff-faced.
His old tweed jacket closely buttoned up,
his gestures careful and deliberate.

We didn't understand what he was teaching us.
It was as if a veil, a gauzy bandage, got between
what he was showing us and what we thought we saw.

He had the air of a gardener, fussily protective
of young seedlings, but we couldn't tell
if he was hiding something or we simply couldn't see it.

At first we noticed there were often scraps of leaves
on the floor where he had stood. Later, thin wisps
of thread like spider's web fell from his jacket.

Finally we grew to understand the work. And on that day
he opened his jacket, which to our surprise
seemed lined with patterned fabric of many shimmering hues

Then he smiled and sighed. And with this movement
the lining rippled and instantly the room was filled
with a flickering storm of swirling butterflies

Dave Calder

REFLECTION

What positive memories do you have of your own teachers?

RETIRING

Our teacher, Mrs Batlow
is leaving this week,
after 40 years of teaching.
So on Friday all of Class 5W
give her a present.
Most of us give her a card
with 'best wishes' but
Sarah presents her with a painting
of Mrs Batlow standing in front of the school.
Emily gives her some flowers.
Nathan gives her a box of chocolates.
Lorenzo gives her a framed photo of Class 5W.
Penny gives her a box of apples!
(Penny's Dad owns a fruit shop.)
Simon gives her a pen in a special case.
Mrs Batlow smiles at each present
and thanks every child
but when Peter gives her his homework
all finished, neat and tidy,
for the first time this year
we all notice that

Mrs Batlow is crying
but
we're not sure if she's happy
or
if she's crying because
she has to mark Peter's homework.

Steven Herrick

IV. NEW EVERY MORNING

from NEW EVERY MORNING

Every day is a fresh beginning;
   Listen, my soul, to the glad refrain,
And, spite of old sorrow and older sinning,
   And puzzles forecasted and possible pain,
   Take heart with the day, and begin again.

               Susan Coolidge

It's hard when you have had a difficult day not to carry the emotions through to the next one. The awkward pupil, the failed lesson. Each day start fresh, a new page, a belief that today you will make a difference . . . and when you do the feeling is like no other.

               Mamaburns, recently retired
               primary teacher

REFLECTION

What gets you up and keeps you going each day?

SOME DAYS

Some days this school
is a huge concrete sandwich
squeezing me out like jam.

It weighs so much
breathing hurts, my legs freeze
my body is heavy.

On days like that
I carry whole buildings
high on my back.

Other days
the school is a rocket
thrusting right into the sun.

It's yellow and green
freshly painted,
the cabin windows
gleam with laughter.

On days like that
whole buildings support me,
my ladder is pushing
over their rooftops.

Amongst the clouds
I'd need a computer
to count all the bubbles
bursting aloud in my head.

David Harmer

Great stuff – to me this is what teaching is like! The intensity and drama of the everyday, the frustration and the stress – but oh, the fun and the satisfaction and the elation!

Primary teacher, Edinburgh

TWENTY BLESSINGS

May the best hour of the day be yours.
May luck go with you from hill to sea.
May you stand against the prevailing wind.
May no forest intimidate you.
May you look out from your own eyes.
May near and far attend you.
May you bathe your face in the sun's rays.
May you have milk, cream, substance.
May your actions be effective.
May your thoughts be affective.
May you will both the wild and the mild.
May you sing the lark from the sky.
May you place yourself in circumstance.
May you be surrounded by goldfinches.
May you pause among alders.
May your desire be infinite.
May what you touch be touched.
May the company be less for your leaving.
May you walk alone beneath the stars.
May your embers still glow in the morning.

Thomas A. Clark

REFLECTION

Create your own blessings to add to the list.

TO BE OF USE

The people I love the best
jump into work head first
without dallying in the shallows
and swim off with sure strokes almost out of sight.
They seem to become natives of that element,
the black sleek heads of seals
bouncing like half-submerged balls.

I love people who harness themselves, an ox to a heavy cart,
who pull like water buffalo, with massive patience,
who strain in the mud and the muck to move things forwards,
who do what has to be done, again and again.

I want to be with people who submerge
in the task, who go into the fields to harvest
and work in a row and pass the bags along,
who are not parlor generals and field deserters
but move in a common rhythm
when the food must come in or the fire be put out.

The work of the world is common as mud.
Botched, it smears the hands, crumbles to dust.
But the thing worth doing well done
has a shape that satisfies, clean and evident.
Greek amphoras for wine or oil,

Hopi vases that held corn, are put in museums
but you know they were made to be used.
The pitcher cries for water to carry
and a person for work that is real.

Marge Piercy

*Teaching offers no option but to jump in and be fully submerged. You
have to be so many things and take many forms, but this is real work.
With great reward.*

S.D., secondary teacher

REFLECTION

What are the qualities you most appreciate in your colleagues?
What do they most appreciate about you?

PLATONIC DIALOGUE

I speak you listen
you speak I listen
I ask you questions
you give me answers
I give you answers
I outline a fact
you repeat the fact
I outline a theory
you question the theory
I tell a laboured joke
you forgive with laughter
you tell a rude joke
I pretend to be shocked
I write on the board
you write in your notebook
I frown you frown
you smile I smile
you chew your pencil
you scratch your temple
I teach you learn
you learn I learn
I fall silent
you fall silent
I get bored with you
you get bored with me

I stifle a yawn
you stifle a laugh
I make you work
you make me work
you read what I've written
I read what you've written
I teach from experience
you learn by experience
I recite what I've memorised
you memorise what I recite
I want you to say it again
you want me to say it again
you learn by heart
I teach by heart
my voice in your ear
my words on your lips
I stay here you go there
your life is there
here your chewed pencil

Gregory Woods

The reciprocal nature of teaching is laid out beautifully here: the biggest successes are the students who surpass you. I often reassure students with 'I'm not smarter than you, I've just had time to learn more'.

Emma Grieve, secondary
English teacher, Orkney

WHAT FIFTY SAID

When I was young my teachers were the old.
I gave up fire for form till I was cold.
I suffered like a metal being cast.
I went to school to age to learn the past.

Now when I am old my teachers are the young.
What can't be molded must be cracked and sprung.
I strain at lessons fit to start a suture.
I go to school to youth to learn the future.

Robert Frost

IN THIS SHORT LIFE

In this short Life
That only lasts an hour
How much – how little – is
Within our power

Emily Dickinson

REFLECTION

What is within your power? What is not?

NOTES ABOUT THE POEMS

'Conversation with the Art Teacher
(a Translation Attempt)' / Raymond Antrobus
This poem was a risk, an attempt to translate BSL
(a signed language with its own rules and syntax as well as
a history of oppression from the hearing/oral world) into
an English language poem (which considers everything I
just mentioned about syntax and history of oppression).
It came out of a face to face interview with my friend
Naimo, a Deaf Art Teacher. I'm not fluent in BSL so I was
using more SSE (sign supported English) to speak with
Naimo who is a BSL native speaker.

'Changed' / Dave Calder
I had been helping a child struggle with homework and got
to thinking on the long process of learning, of the moment
of 'getting it', of the satisfaction and release at reaching that
understanding to both pupil and teacher – like something
growing and hatching, I thought . . .

'Twenty Blessings' / Thomas A. Clark
In traditional societies it was a common practice to offer
blessings and short prayers on almost any occasion, for the

success of the occasion or for the well-being of the company. A few lines of 'Twenty Blessings' are taken directly from the *Carmina Gadelica*, a collection of material from the Gaelic oral tradition.

'Slow Reader' / Vicki Feaver
This poem, one of the first I ever wrote, was about my son. The Ladybird book was the reader he brought home from his primary school. A couple of months later he was given a book that really excited him and he was soon reading fluently on his own. For me the poem is partly about a child who has been put off reading by finding books rather dull; partly about the feeling that a child, like a colt, needs to run free for a time and enjoy themselves.

It was also, I think, a bit about me. I was a 'slow poet'. I wanted to be a poet as a child but didn't have the courage to write until I was in my mid-thirties.

'How to Be a Teacher' / Rebecca Lynne Fullan
I wrote this poem after my first year of teaching. During that year, I felt like I was failing every time I walked in the classroom. About halfway through, I realised that failure, in terms of being pushed out beyond what I knew confidently, was the condition of teaching well.

'Some Days' / David Harmer
I wrote this poem quite a long time ago when I was a primary-school teacher. I knew that for some of the children, school wasn't great some days, and on other days it was really exciting! I also knew that it was the same for me and teachers everywhere. We all bring stuff in our heads to school which can make it a bad day but very often being with our friends and doing things we really like can make going to school fantastic. In fact, most days it is like that. But on some days . . .

'Retiring' / Steven Herrick
When my sons were children, each afternoon they would eagerly tell me about their school day. They knew I'd turn their memories into poems. They were generous in allowing a house-bound poet to leave his desk and wander with them through the classroom and schoolyard. It was the best journey of my life.

'A Book Closer to Home' / Nabila Jameel
This poem has emerged from my weekly visits on a Saturday to the local library with my mum. It addresses the idea of 'woman' before 'mother', the loss of language, the finding of peace and contentment in the written form of the mother tongue; and the harsh dominance of the superior language.

'Fear of the Litany' / Maggie Kazel

My first year gave me such a wake-up call – realising I loved kids and teaching. But being lesbian there in such a 'straight' environment was almost too much. A veteran teacher – Terry – was my unofficial mentor. Sharing my fear with him broke my paralyzing silence – all new teachers deserve their own Terry.

'Every line is imaginary' / William Letford

I'd watched my nephew racing for his school. I felt I was running with him. It reminded me of all the finishing lines, deadlines, aims, targets, and goals that had risen up and fallen away. How important they seem and insignificant they become. I wanted to shout, *keep going, you'll be okay*.

'Listen' / Liz Lochhead

I'm glad this poem has been chosen for this anthology because teachers will, I hope, recognise and empathise with the speaker of the poem. A boy of about 14 or 15, I think – though could be a particularly sullen and troubled girl? It seems everyone needs reminding that the 'I' speaking a poem is not necessarily the poet. I've always enjoyed using 'impoverished' clichés in a playful way because I love listening to colloquial speech. The irony is, this silent, or silenced, voice is only able to articulate itself within the impossible world of the poem.

'Sam but different / Same but different' /
Christine De Luca
Growing up bilingual – Shetlandic and English – I gradually
came to appreciate the joys of linguistic flexibility.
Languages open doors into apparently different worlds,
but stepping further in, the differences fade away in our
common humanity. I try to help children value their mother
tongue but also to enjoy learning other languages.

'clann a cluich, sgoil achadh nan sian' / 'children playing,
   achnasheen school' / Aonghas Macneacail
As a writer, I have visited many schools. Each is, in its own
way, a means of rediscovering your own childhood, into
which the experiences of all the intervening years may be
fed. The essence is to revisit and marry that knowledge with
a retained sense of innocence.

'Hamid' / Rowland Molony
How to tackle Shakespeare in school? 'Hamid' is a brief
look at the gap between young people and 400 year-
old Shakespeare. Shakespeare has cracking stories and
magnetic characters. In teaching him, story is primary,
language secondary. First get into the drama, then the
brilliance of the words.

'Classroom Politics' / Fiona Norris
This poem was written way back in the early 1980s when I was a young English teacher, keen to make a real difference to my pupils, both in their learning and in their lives. This simple poem expresses the sense of responsibility I felt, particularly towards the girls.

'School of Embodied Poetics' / Nina Pick
I wrote this poem when I was struggling with my role as a teacher in a university, higher education in general being a place where intellectualism is privileged and embodiment and intuition – more feminine ways of knowing – are discounted. I was just learning how to stand in front of a classroom as a shy person, as a person with a body, and be authentic, rather than hide behind a mask or a persona. I ultimately came to the decision that I wanted to model a kind of honesty or integrity to my students, that a way of being could also be a way of teaching.

'Platonic Dialogue' / Gregory Woods
I taught in universities. My career began with plenty of work in personal tutorials and small seminar groups. It ended with distance-learning packs and lectures to crowds of people who weren't necessarily even in the same room. Teaching should be an intimate conversation, with love and respect on both sides.

ACKNOWLEDGEMENTS

Our thanks are due to the following authors, publishers, and estates who have generously given permission to reproduce works. We have endeavoured to contact and clear permissions with all poets and publishers listed here; if there are any omissions, please contact the Scottish Poetry Library.

Allan Ahlberg, 'Glenis', from *Please Mrs Butler* (Puffin, 2013), copyright © Allan Ahlberg, 1984, reproduced by permission of Penguin Books Ltd; Raymond Antrobus, 'Conversation with the Art Teacher (A Translation Attempt)' from *The Perseverance* (Penned in the Margins, 2018), by permission of the publisher; James Berry, 'Isn't My Name Magical' and 'People Equal' from *A Story I Am In: Selected Poems* (Bloodaxe Books, 2011), reproduced with permission of Bloodaxe Books; Wendell Berry, 'The Peace of Wild Things' from *New Collected Poems*, © 2012 by Wendell Berry. Reprinted by permission of Counterpoint Press; Dave Calder, 'Changed' from *Dolphins Leap Lampposts* (Macmillan Children's, 2002), by permission of the author; Thomas A. Clark, 'Twenty Blessings' (Moschatel Press, 1999), by permission of the author; Billy Collins, 'On Turning Ten' from *The Art of*

Woodwick Mill: Orkney Poems in Scots (Grace Note, 2015), by permission of the publisher; Miroslav Holub, 'A boy's head' and 'The door' from *Poems Before & After: Collected English Translations*, trans. Ian & Jarmila Milner et al. (Bloodaxe Books, 2006), reproduced with permission of Bloodaxe Books, www.bloodaxebooks.com; Nabila Jameel, 'A Book Closer To Home' by permission of the author; Peter Kahn, 'On First Knowing You're a Teacher' from *Little Kings* (Nine Arches Press, 2020) by permission of the publisher; Jackie Kay, 'Duncan Gets Expelled' from *Two's Company* (Blackie, 1994). Copyright © Jackie Kay, 1994, reproduced by permission of Penguin Books Ltd; Maggie Kazel, 'Fear of the Litany' by permission of the author; William Letford, 'Every line is imaginary' from *Dirt* (Carcanet Press, 2016), by permission of the publisher; Ada Limón, 'Instructions on Not Giving Up' from *The Carrying* (Minneapolis: Milkweed Editions, 2018), copyright © 2018 by Ada Limón. Reprinted with permission from Milkweed Editions, milkweed.org; Liz Lochhead, 'Listen' from *Fugitive Colours* (Polygon, 2016), reproduced with permission of the Licensor through PLSclear; aonghas macneacail, 'clann a cluich, sgoil achadh nan sian/ children playing, achnasheen school' by permission of the author; Hugh McMillan, 'End Of Year Exam', from *Not Actually Being In Dumfries* (Luath Press, 2015), by permission of the author; Rowland Molony, 'Hamid', by permission of the author; Kim Moore, 'Leaving Teaching', by permission

of the author; Pat Mora, 'Ode to Teachers', copyright ©
2010 by Pat Mora, originally appeared in *Dizzy In Your
Eyes*, published by Alfred A. Knopf, reprinted by permission
of Curtis Brown, Ltd; Partaw Naderi, 'My Voice' – original
Farsi-Dari poem by Partaw Naderi; English translation
by Sarah Maguire and Yama Yari. Poem copyright ©
Partaw Naderi 2008; translation copyright © The Poetry
Translation Centre 2008. Reprinted with permission;
Fiona Norris, 'Classroom Politics', by permission of
the author; Nina Pick, 'School of Embodied Poetics', by
permission of the author; Marge Piercy, 'To be of use',
copyright ©1973, 1982 by Marge Piercy from *Circles on the
Water* (Alfred A. Knopf), used by permission of The Wallace
Literary Agency; Eveline Pye, 'Scaffolding' by permission
of the author; Wisława Szymborska, 'Four A.M.' from
Poems New And Collected 1957-1997, translated from the
Polish by Stanisław Barańczak and Clare Cavanagh.
English translation copyright © 1998 by Houghton Mifflin
Harcourt Publishing Company. Used by permission of
Houghton Mifflin Harcourt Publishing Company; and
'Czwarta nad ranem' from Calling out to Yeti, 1957 /
Wołanie do Yeti, (Znak, 2017), by permission of the
publisher; Gael Turnbull, 'Lines for a Bookmark' from
There Are Words: Collected Poems (Shearsman Books, 2006),
by permission of Jill Turnbull; Tom Wayman, 'Did I Miss
Anything?' from *Did I Miss Anything? Selected Poems 1973–
1993* (Harbour Publishing, 1993), copyright © 1993 Tom

Wayman. All rights reserved. Reprinted by permission of Harbour Publishing; Gregory Woods, 'Platonic Dialogue' by permission of the author. We are also glad to have permission to reproduce 'Sometimes'.

With thanks to all the teachers who wrote in response to particular poems:

Kate Hendry (secondary teacher), Richard (primary teacher), Angela Bell (DHT Secondary), Andrea Bradley (former secondary teacher), Jane Cooper (former secondary teacher, Edinburgh), Mamaburns (recently retired primary teacher), S.D. (secondary teacher), and Emma Grieve (secondary English teacher, Orkney).